A Beginner's G

The Garden Series

Dueep J. Singh

Mendon Cottage Books

JD-Biz Publishing

All Rights Reserved.

No part of this publication may be reproduced in any form or by any means, including scanning, photocopying, or otherwise without prior written permission from JD-Biz Corp Copyright © 2014

All Images Licensed by Fotolia and 123RF. Line illustrations and sketches by DJS.

Disclaimer

The information is this book is provided for informational purposes only. It is not intended to be used and medical advice or a substitute for proper medical treatment by a qualified health care provider. The information is believed to be accurate as presented based on research by the author.

The contents have not been evaluated by the U.S. Food and Drug Administration or any other Government or Health Organization and the contents in this book are not to be used to treat cure or prevent disease.

The author or publisher is not responsible for the use or safety of any diet, procedure or treatment mentioned in this book. The author or publisher is not responsible for errors or omissions that may exist.

Warning

The Book is for informational purposes only and before taking on any diet, treatment or medical procedure, it is recommended to consult with your primary health care provider.

Our books are available at
1. Amazon.com
2. Barnes and Noble
3. Itunes
4. Kobo
5. Smashwords
6. Google Play Books

Table of Contents

Introduction to Rock Gardens 1

    Introduction 4

        Wrong Way Of Placing Rocks 13

        The Right Way to Place Rock Stones 13

        Good Rock Work- 13

        Flat Ground 13

        Wall 15

        Stones on Slopes 16

    Choosing the Best Soil 18
    Building Your Rock Garden 20
    Planting Your Rock Plants 22
    Maintenance 25
    Conifers 28
    Bulbs 31
    List of Rock Plants, depending on the Particular Conditions and Places 33
        Rock Plants For Walls 34

        Crazy paving plants – 34

    Conclusion 35
    Author Bio 36
    Publisher 47

Introduction

Rock gardens have been part of landscaping and gardening lore for millenniums. In the East Japanese rock gardens or Zen gardens have been places where people could meditate in serene and harmonious surroundings.

Why are more people designing their own gardens incorporating at least one rock garden in the design? Even if the rock garden is quite small, it is going to add a touch of distinction to the landscaping of your garden.

In Japan, rock gardens were normally built as dry landscape gardens, where a number of landscapes were made up of natural compositions made from natural products incorporated into a landscape. These natural items included bushes, trees, Moss, water, rocks and sand. One believes that the concept of rock gardening originated in China, especially when the ancient religion of Shintoism spoke about places of harmony where one could commune with nature and the spirit in serenity. These were normally made in monasteries, where they could be seen from one focal point, like say the porch of the head priest of the monastery.

These dry Landscape gardens which you call a Zen garden in Japan were built to be seen from one viewpoint, with the walling closed around it in ancient times. Nowadays they stretch on for miles incorporating all the natural features available and present in the area to make up harmonious surroundings.

Japanese Zen gardens go back to 784 BC. Chinese gardens have been around for even longer. The incorporation of gravel and white sand in a Zen or rock garden was an important feature. These were the symbol of distance, emptiness, purity, white space and water. All these symbols were supposed to aid in meditation. White sand and gravel used harmoniously together were also used around temples, shrines and palaces.

Choosing the Right Site

A great deal is going to depend on the position or the shape of the ground. A sunny site is always welcome which means that you can grow plants there which enjoy the sun. As many of the plants which are planted here are alpine plants, any site which has unrestricted light is going to be welcome.

Secondly, the site should be in a place where the garden is made into a separate feature. Don't make it right in the middle of your lawn, because that is going to distract from the beauty of a well-kept lawn. Don't make it around a fountain or an artificial landscaping feature because that is going to distract from the originality of the design.

Even a belt of shrubs planted on purpose is better as a division that having no separation at all between other features and your rock garden.

Never plan a rock garden near Sycamore trees or elm trees. These are not very common in these, and that is why gardeners and horticulturists did not bother much about these particular trees have on the soil affecting the growth of the plants in your rockery.

In fact, I would suggest don't make any sort of rock garden near any large tree. That is because these large trees are going to send out their roots tremendous distances underground and so rob your plants of food and moisture.

When you are choosing the site, look for a site which has a slight slope. This is excellent because you are now going to be placing the rocks naturally. This also produces more pleasing aesthetic affects. Also a little bit of slope means that water is not going to get waterlogged in the soil, but is going to run down the slope or get absorbed into the soil.

If the ground is not variable in contour, you can make an attempt by breaking up the outline. This is done by forming mounds of earth and by putting the stone into suitable positions.

This reminds me of one of my gardening addict relatives, who was getting her house renovated. The contractors in the East have this bad tendency of breaking up the house and not removing the debris. That means all that broken up stone, cement and other building materials used in the construction of a new portion of your house are going to be there littering your garden or your surroundings until you ask somebody else to pick it up and lug it away.

She was a gardening enthusiast, and looked at all those mounds of eyesores disfiguring her garden. And then she noticed that the piles had more of soil and earth instead of man-made cement and other artificial building materials. She immediately dispatched her husband with the car to the nearest mountainside where he was requested to pick up a number of colorful rocks and stones.

Try hunting for these near river beds.

And now her garden has three amazingly beautiful rock gardens. Nobody can say that they originated with piles of disfiguring mud left over on a construction site.

The next point, she did was to make the path below the natural level of the soil. That meant that we had to look up to the garden, especially when it looked like a mini mountain full of rocks and beautiful plants.

Rock and Stone Placement

The different types of stones which you can use in the paving or placing in your garden are going to be in five different traditional modes. They are either going to be flat or declining. They are going to be tall and vertical or small and vertical. And the last option is arching rocks.

These rocks are going to be sedimentary rocks, especially those found by mountainsides, seashores and rivers. You can also use igneous rocks to create mountains. If the rock does not look very well on one side, just place it leaning and smother with plants.

The most suitable rock material is what you are going to find in nature. Not all of us are plutocrats, and we are definitely not going to be spending thousands of dollars in buying made to order stones and rocks brought from long distances.

For example, some places you can get really beautiful weathered limestone and sandstone. You can also use granite. When I was at university I was living in an area where slabs of granite were harvested from the mountains. I was fascinated by the beautiful fossilized ferns being excavated everyday by these Philistine contractors who could not care less about the delicate tracery of Mica, making up those exquisite pieces of natural fossils.

I did not have a garden of my own at that time because I was living in the University hostel. But that did not stop me from carrying home lots and lots of pieces of these beautiful rock fossils for our garden, during our annual holidays.

Unfortunately, as things go, we were transferred out and father did not want to lug all of those heavy pieces of rock to a place 2000 miles away, notwithstanding the priceless fossils in them. So there they stand and here is to hoping that the new tenants appreciated a fossilized granite rock garden. I do not think so. These fossils are so common in many areas of the country that they are considered to be a part of the landscape!

Remember that a granite slab is not going to absorb moisture very well. That is why it does not encourage the plants to cling to it.

The fairly soft stones can make a pleasant contrast to your landscape. But do not choose such stone which is easily damaged and which flakes easily in frosty weather. I was surprised to see some of the stones that I had collected during forays into the hills and mountains suddenly cracking after an unexpectedly cold spell. I was rather perplexed – these stones had come from the mountains, how come they cracked in the winter in the plains.

My uncle gave me an explanation that there was some moisture inside the stone which caused it to crack. As an explanation, it does as well as any other reason. Also, I noticed that he was not using all that lovely leftover marble from the building project. He said that this stone was definitely not natural, especially when it was polished and shined up artificially. Brickbats and concrete are also not aesthetically pleasing at all.

So the leftover marble was used in the making of stone seats in a place away from the rock garden. But it did not disturb the natural harmony of suitably placed stones.

http://www.123rf.com/photo_19244917_the-world-famous-zen-garden-at-ryoan-ji-temple-during-early-april-in-kyoto-japan.html

More horizontally placed stones are going to have a more attractive aesthetic effect than vertically placed stones. Traditionally, these rocks are rarely placed in symmetrical designs or straight patterns and lines. That is because this is not a true natural placement of rocks. You are trying to create something which imitates nature, but in a more harmonious manner. Some basic combinations are going to include one large rock and two accompanying rocks or one tall and vertical rock next to a flat or reclining rock.

The rocks that you are going to choose are going to be varied in color. I remember accompanying my uncle on these rock hunting trips to the mountains and making a beeline for rocks with striated colors. He had to do the picking up and he started to get a bit annoyed, because some of them were very beautiful, but they were so heavy!

Nevertheless, we persevered and got those rocks for the rock gardens, and they are just there for show with no plants around them. We just sit on them, and contemplate the butterflies in the garden!

A little bit of harmony is not going to be disturbed with a little bit of spontaneity, so you can scatter some of these rocks as if all unknowinglike, throughout the garden.

Gravel is not disturbed very much by the wind and the rain and that is what makes it a better landscaping choice than sand.

Do not attempt anything very elaborate in your small garden. See that the rocks are natural by all means, and try to give them height by planting an evergreen shrub or two at one point or another. You can have the highest point at one end and a point which is not quite so high at the other end. The intervening space is going to be undulating naturally, but do not make it too symmetrical.

Wrong Way Of Placing Rocks

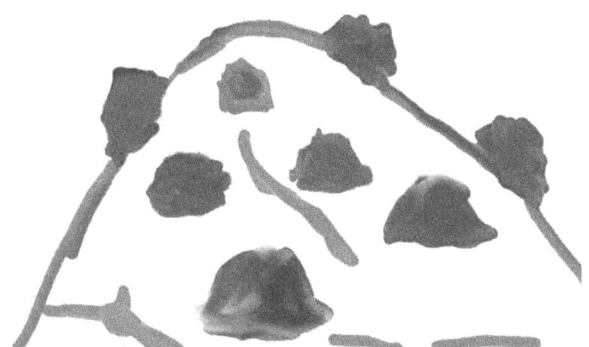

Small stones or rocks placed haphazardly are not going to add style to your budding garden. The stones should be, if possible, at least 2 feet in length. They should also be about the same breadth to stop.

The Right Way to Place Rock Stones

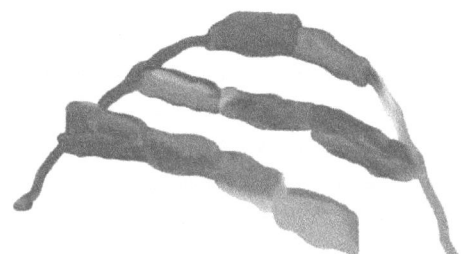

Good Rock Work-

Flat Ground

This is how stones, rocks and pebbles are normally placed on a flat surface in a lying down position.

Wall

The stones are embedded in the wall with soil placed between them and the plants growing in between the rock hollows.

Stones on Slopes

Choosing the Best Soil

Now that we have set the rocks on the site, it is time to choose the best soil for our plants. There are plenty of amateur gardeners who still consider soil to be one of those dirty, grimy masses of earth which is such a bore to handle.

Remember this soil is definitely not an inert dry, crumbly mass which gets to become such a muddy mess after some rainfall. Instead, it is this soil, which is going to be the place where your roots are going to grow. This soil anchors your plants down. This is the soil which has all the essential nutrients which are going to help your plants flourish thanks to the bacteria which live in this soil.

Millions of living organisms – bless them – are busy converting nutritional items present in the soil into food forms which are beneficial to your plant. If these bacteria were not present here, the soil would be as sterile as it is on Mars or is on the moon. As we are out to get the best out of our garden, we need to encourage this bacteria with might and main. That can be done by aerating the soil. It can also be done by giving the soil plenty of water.

It is possible that you are using the soil already in your garden as a basis for making the garden features. You may also be using soil from previous excavations in making undulations and mounds.

Nevertheless, it is always a good experiment to try out different types of soils in different portions so that you can grow special plants there. It is possible, the natural soil in your garden is too heavy or too damp.

So you cannot grow succulent plants in that particular area, where there is plenty of water, and because they like totally dry soil with low water content.

Your soil may also contain far too little of natural nutrients and that is why it needs plenty of organic fertilizer. Look at the plants which you are going to grow. What are the needs which are going to help them flourish? Do they like too much of limestone? Are you growing alpine plants? Just make some pockets in your garden with calcareous soil or the soil best suited to your choice of plants.

These pockets may contain only 18 inches of soil. But they should have enough of place for the roots to run under the top 18 inches. A good general mixture is going to be eight parts of ordinary garden soil mixed with half a part of coarse sand and half a part of rock chippings.

Leaf mold needs to be added to this soil if it is of a heavy, water retaining and clayey character.

Just before you do the planting other materials can be incorporated. These include Peat for some plants, sand for other plants and more Leaf mold for a third group of plants and so on.

Do not forget that some Alpines like a good deal of crushed limestone or granite. This is granite is going to suit plants that dislike line in any form. *Campanula alpestris* also known as the Alpine Bellflower is one of these plants. The *Androsace* species is a dwarf Alpine, belonging to the Primula family. This has a cluster of pinkish purplish flowers which looks very attractive when grown in a granite based soil. They also like more than a quarter of the compost to consist of grit. When you are planting saxifrages, you can use ordinary loam.

Gentians like peat, as do *Primulas* [Cow Slips] and *Lithospermums*.

Building Your Rock Garden

Always start building at the lowest point by bedding the base rocks in the ground. They should be put in sufficiently deeply. At least two thirds of the rocks should be buried to make them look just like a natural outcrop. They will thus incline towards the main body of the soil in which they rest.

The tilting backwards slightly is going to help to guide the rain down to the roots of the plants and not to take it away as the other rocks are placed into position, they may either have a tilt the right or to the left.

Whatever tilt is given to the lower stones, the higher ones should follow the same sequence for a good distance. You can consider this to be a theme of natural stratification.

As the stones are put into position suitable soil may be placed behind them and rammed tightly to keep them in position. Do not forget the pockets which may be as large as 3 ft.^{2}, even if the large ones have smaller rocks peeping through them.

Your priority is to make it look natural. So do not build pinnacle like effects, which is definitely not a natural feature. There is no reason why grass should not form a part of your garden scheme. Moss is always welcome. In fact, stone outcroppings from grass look fascinating and natural.

Even in a small rock garden, see that certain stones have a flat surface to act as stepping stones for getting about from place to place. Do not make them of marble, because as I said before marble has an artificial feel. Try granite or flat igneous rocks.

Whatever you do, make sure that rocks and stones do not stick out of the surface like decorative dry fruit in a custard or trifle!

Planting Your Rock Plants

Once you have made your garden, your next priority is to see it carpeted and furnished at the earliest possible moment. There are a number of plants which are going to do this really quickly, but because they are strong, growing, they are apt to smother weaker and choicer plants in consequence.

So make sure that you do not overdo the strong growers. Once you have planted them see that they are cut back and trimmed regularly and keep them within bounds. I have seen lots of these ambitious projects starting out with a choice selection of plants, only to end up a year or two later, just a mass of one or two of the most dominant and rampant types, growing all over the place.

The best quick growing plants, which you can grow are Iberis, [Candy tuft] Arabis, [Rock Cress or Alpine Rock Cress] Cerastium, [Mouse Ear Chickweed] Aubretia, [Purple Cascade] and Alyssum saxatile [Basket of Gold]. However, these plants have to be kept in control, otherwise they are going to take over your rockery.

You can do with the planting any time in the autumn or in the spring providing the ground is fit to work and has been prepared beforehand with organic fertilizer and the rocks placed in position.

As this garden is going to be at its best late in the spring, an autumn planting is preferable on the whole.

Now let us concentrate on the likes and dislikes of the plants we are going to grow. Some of the common species are Primula; they like lots of moisture and so they should be planted in the lower positions and near water. If you have a small pool so much the better. However, if you are planting Sedum [Purple Emperor] or Sempervivum [Hens and Chicks] they are definitely not going to flourish in soil full of moisture because they are succulents and prefer dry soil. Too much of moisture is going to rot them.

In the same manner, plants of the Dianthus family prefer lots of sun, while Oxalis likes shades.

That means you are not going to be planting your plants just about anywhere. You will need to see where they like to grow and where they can get all the necessary nutrients and resources to flourish and bloom in your garden.

Plant your plants firmly in the soil so that the roots can get a sturdy grip. Make a hole with a trowel. Put the plant into position so that it is at the right level. Firm the soil all around it after the plant has been planted. You may want to sprinkle some water on the soil and tamp it down.

See that there is no hollow beneath the plant before you press down all around the base of the roots. There is a great danger when you are planting between clefts of rock of the loosening of soil at the base in this case it is better to ram the soil into position, first of all making certain that is sufficiently open by putting some gritty material in with the compost.

Do not plant too deeply so as to bury the plant, but on the other hand, see that the roots are not left out of the soil in a high and dry position.

Maintenance

Apart from the nutrition which your plants are going to get through organic fertilizer, you may need to do forking and raking occasionally. These are designed to get the soil down to a fine condition suitable either for the sewing of seeds or the putting out of plants. This fine soil is known as tilth.

In the autumn, a gardener digs the ground to as deeper depth as possible, leaving the land rough and in the spring and the early summer, he aims to get a fine tilth.

People normally use rakes which are designed to prepare the land for sowing the seed, making designs in the gravel – this is done in Zen gardens – or just for shifting the soil so that it can get aerated.

The rake is drawn backwards and forwards over the surface of the ground leaving the land in a fine condition and absolutely level. Rakes are normally not used for removing large quantity of small stones. Leave these stones in because they are going to assist in the drainage. They are also going to help in the movement of the air.

In the summer, these stones tend to keep the land cool. The surface stones act as a mulch. In the winter they are going to keep your land warmer. So do not waste your time in raking your land continually for the purpose of stone removal.

Make sure that you keep weeding regularly during the year. The weekly deweeding of the weeds between your plants is a necessary procedure so that the nutrients do not get grabbed by the weeds.

This usually means going over the garden about once in a fortnight stirring the soil with a little fork and removing the weeds by hand. Such regular attention is going to take only half an hour or so in your garden, and it is going to save hours of labor later on.

When we were young, the rather tyrannical head gardener had this bad habit of giving us a fork all in the name of teaching us how to garden and getting us to do the weed removal while he lazed about.

For a couple of days we were very enthusiastic about this, till we found out that this was his way of delegating his work on to our shoulders while he chewed a plug of tobacco and meditated under the nearest fruit tree.

So we, being rather nasty little kidlet specimens got together *all the weeds* collected by the two workers/helpers as well as what we had done throughout the day, and welcomed our father that evening with "look what we have done today. We did the deweeding, like we did yesterday and the day before."

Father saw and cogitated. His kids were not going to be workhorses doing the job allocated to a gardener who was not earning an honest day's pay.

The head gardener was immediately shunted off to another officer's garden and a much more genial and hard-working real gardener was sent to us. And he taught us how to make rock gardens and how to make real compost heaps.

We enjoyed that last thoroughly! Kids do, especially when they are given activities involving lots of dirt, soil, greenery and the scope of getting thoroughly grimy and dirty.

The moment the groups of plants have flowered, they are going to need attending to. All the dead flowers and stems should be cut off. The stronger growing types should be cut back to prevent them from spoiling other plants. Also, they need to be kept in control.

Early in February, depending on the frost and the weather, you can remove the straggling growths from the brown patches of Aubretia or Saxifrage. These plants are going to look brown and nearly dead, but they are going to revive again in the spring. A little soil shifted on the top is excellent top dressing. You can also fork some organic fertilizer here and there lightly.

Many of the early flowering types are going to have their buds damaged by birds, especially when they are in the budding stage. You will need to protect them by placing little pieces of wood twigs pushed in around the plants with strands of black cotton stretched in between them.

Some plants are apt to die during the winter, not that much because of the frost, but because of the damp. These should be covered with a small piece of glass before the winter starts, if you are living in an area subject to harsh frosts.

The plants which you are going to treat in this manner include Androsaces and the less hardy Hens and chicks, which are succulents. Succulents originally were native in areas with less of water and less of frost, so the next time you feel a frost coming in, put some glass over your plants.

Conifers

These are excellent for potting, too!

If you want to get a Japanese garden or Lilliputian effect in your garden, there is nothing that helps more than the planting of conifers. These are in themselves perfect in shape, and yet they never grow to any large size.

You may want to buy conifers that keep small as they will then be always in keeping with your Alpine plants.

Here are some suitable varieties which I would suggest –

Cupressus obtusa var caespitosa – this produces mosslike dense effects. The growth is rounded.

Cupressus plumosa aurea compacta – this is golden in color, miniature and cone shaped. Very popular in Japanese gardens.

Juniperus communis compressa – small and column like neat conifers.

Picea Albertiana conica – these are pyramidal in shape and grow very slowly. They like moist soil and a sheltered position.

Taxus baccata pygmaea – dwarf varieties and beautiful green in color

Taxus compacta – slow-growing and compact

Thuya occidentalis Ellwangeriana Aurea – Golden pyramidal bush

Thuya plicata aurea Rogersii – pyramidal in form with gold and bronze foliage

Ulex nanus– dwarf gorse which flowers in September.

Bulbs

Bulbs are definitely a welcome addition anywhere in a garden, especially those which growing light soil and which can be planted in the depth suitable for the size of the bulb. Different types of bulbs and varieties can be obtained, which are going to flower at different periods of the year.

A few examples of the most popular bulb varieties are given here –

Spring flowering bulbs – Allium in variety, Anemone in variety, Crocus, Chionodoxa, Fritillaria , Iris, Scilla, Tulips and Muscari.

Summer flowering bulbs – Allium pulchellum, Oxalis floribunda, tritonia crocata etc.

Autumn Flowering Bulbs – crocus, Cyclamen africanum, Cyclamen europium, Cyclamen Neapolitanum, Scilla autumnalis

Winter Flowering Bulbs – anemone, crocus, Galanthus, Iris – different varieties.

This particular website has an excellent list of all the other bulbs which you can find in your area and you can plant according to the climate and your wish.

http://www.flowerpowerfundraising.com/customer-service/plants/rock-garden-collection

List of Rock Plants, depending on the Particular Conditions and Places

This list is also going to be short, because one can just give a gardener an outline of all the plants which can be planted, and the conditions particular to them. You may want to go online or consult an experienced nursery professional to give you more advice on these particular plants and others.

Shade loving plants –

These plants consist of Ferns, Aconites, primulas, Androsace oliosa, Arinaria balearica, Ramondia etc.

Plants Which like Half Shade –

Primulas, Androsace arachnoidea, Aster alpinus, saxifrage, viola, epigaea, Mertensia, etc.

Plants Which like Moisture –

Trillium, Mimulus Parnassia etc.

Rock Plants Which Dislike the Damp –

You will need to cover them with a piece of glass, a few inches above in winter – Androsace, Campanula Artemisia, Dianthus, Papaver Alpenum.

Rock Plants For Walls –

Alyssum, saponaria, Iberis, Dianthus, Aubretia, Corydalis, Linaria etc.

Crazy paving plants –

Sedum lydium, Alyssum montanum, Dianthus deltoidis, Erinus alpinus, Mints and peppermints, Thyme, etc.

D.Deltoides- Maiden Pink.

You can also look for a list of other plants on this excellent URL –

http://landscaping.about.com/od/waterfeaturerockgarden/tp/Rock-Garden-Plants.htm

Conclusion

This book has given you a beginner's introduction to construction of a rock garden, which is going to give you plenty of pleasure as it grows. You do not have to go in for classical styles and designs, if you are looking for just an unusual feature in your garden landscape. Apart from this, these gardens can be made in a limited area and can become very attractive features to entice you during your daily promenade in your garden.

So it does not matter whether you are an experienced gardener or an immature hobbyist – start collecting rocks and stones for your rock garden right now.

Live Long and Prosper!

Author Bio

Dueep Jyot Singh is a Management and IT Professional who managed to gather Postgraduate qualifications in Management and English and Degrees in Science, French and Education while pursuing different enjoyable career options like being an hospital administrator, IT,SEO and HRD Database Manager/ trainer, movie , radio and TV scriptwriter, theatre artiste and public speaker, lecturer in French, Marketing and Advertising, ex-Editor of Hearts On Fire (now known as Solstice) Books Missouri USA, advice columnist and cartoonist, publisher and Aviation School trainer, ex-moderator on Medico.in, banker, student councilor ,travelogue writer … among other things!

One fine morning, she decided that she had enough of killing herself by Degrees and went back to her first love -- writing. It's more enjoyable! She already has 48 published academic and 14 fiction- in- different- genre books under her belt.

When she is not designing websites or making Graphic design illustrations for clients , she is browsing through old bookshops hunting for treasures, of which she has an enviable collection – including R.L. Stevenson, O.Henry, Dornford Yates, Maurice Walsh, De Maupassant, Victor Hugo, Sapper, C.N. Williamson, "Bartimeus" and the crown of her collection- Dickens "The Old Curiosity Shop," and so on… Just call her "Renaissance Woman") - collecting herbal remedies, acting like Universal Helping Hand/Agony Aunt, or escaping to her dear mountains for a bit of exploring, collecting herbs and plants and trekking.

Check out some of the other JD-Biz Publishing books

Gardening Series on Amazon

Health Learning Series

- THE MAGIC OF GOOSEBERRIES FOR HEALTH AND BEAUTY
- THE MAGIC OF YOGURT FOR COOKING AND BEAUTY
- THE MAGIC OF LEMONS USING LEMONS FOR HEALTH AND BEAUTY
- THE MAGIC OF CHILLIES FOR COOKING AND HEALING
- THE MAGIC OF ONIONS ONIONS IN CUISINE TO CURE AND TO HEAL
- THE MAGIC OF RADISHES TO CURE AND TO HEAL
- THE MAGIC OF CARROTS TO CURE AND TO HEAL
- THE HEALTH BENEFITS OF OREGANO FOR COOKING AND HEALTH
- The Magic Of MARIGOLDS Marigolds for Health And Beauty
- THE HEALTH BENEFITS OF CINNAMON
- THE MAGIC OF COCONUTS FOR COOKING & HEALTH
- THE MAGIC OF CLOVES FOR HEALING AND COOKING
- THE MAGIC OF ASAFETIDA FOR COOKING AND HEALING
- THE MAGIC OF NEEM MARGOSA TO HEAL
- THE MAGIC OF SALT TO HEAL AND FOR BEAUTY
- THE MAGIC OF POMEGRANATES FOR HEALTH AND BEAUTY
- THE MAGIC OF DRY FRUIT AND SPICES REMEDIES AND RECIPES
- THE HEALTH BENEFITS OF TURMERIC CURCUMIN FOR COOKING AND HEALTH
- THE MAGIC OF VEGETABLES ANCIENT HEALING REMEDIES AND TIPS / THE MAGIC OF ALOE VERA
- THE HEALTH BENEFITS OF ROSEMARY FOR COOKING AND HEALTH
- THE MAGIC OF PEPPER & PEPPERCORNS FOR COOKING & HEALING
- THE MAGIC OF MILK, BUTTER AND CHEESE FOR COOKING & HEALING
- THE MAGIC OF CARDAMOMS FOR COOKING AND HEALTH
- THE HEALTH BENEFITS OF BLACK CUMIN FOR COOKING AND HEALTH
- THE MAGIC OF BASIL-TULSI TO HEAL NATURALLY
- THE MAGIC OF SPICES FOR HEALTH AND CUISINE
- THE MAGIC OF ROSES FOR COOKING AND BEAUTY
- The Miraculous Healing Powers of GINGER
- The Miracle of HONEY

Country Life Books

GRANDMA'S
NATURAL REMEDIES AND ANCIENT HERBAL BEAUTY RECIPES
Volume 1
HEALTH LEARNING SERIES
DLJEEP J SINGH AND J DAVIDSON
GRANDMA'S
NATURAL REMEDIES AND ANCIENT HERBAL BEAUTY RECIPES
Volume 2
HEALTH LEARNING SERIES
DLJEEP J SINGH AND J DAVIDSON
GRANDMA'S
NATURAL REMEDIES AND ANCIENT RECIPES
GRANDMA'S CURE FOR OBESITY
GRANDMA'S CURE FOR THE COMMON COLD
Volume 3
HEALTH LEARNING SERIES
DLJEEP J SINGH AND J DAVIDSON
GRANDMA'S
NATURAL REMEDIES AND ANCIENT HERBAL RECIPES
Volume 4
HEALTH LEARNING SERIES
DLJEEP J SINGH AND J DAVIDSON
GRANDMA'S
HERBAL LORE
ANCIENT HERBAL RECIPES AND REMEDIES
Volume 5
HEALTH LEARNING SERIES
DLJEEP J SINGH AND J DAVIDSON
GRANDMA'S
ANCIENT BEAUTY REMEDIES FROM HER KITCHEN
Volume 6
HEALTH LEARNING SERIES
DLJEEP J SINGH AND J DAVIDSON
GRANDMA'S
EASY TO USE TIPS
IN THE KITCHEN AND OUTDOORS
Volume 7
HEALTH LEARNING SERIES
DLJEEP J SINGH AND J DAVIDSON
GRANDMA'S
HOUSEHOLD HINTS AND RECIPES
USING TIME TESTED ECONOMICAL TIPS IN YOUR HOME
75 Tips
Remove Stains
Peel Tomatoes
Perfect Pies
HEALTH LEARNING SERIES
DLJEEP J SINGH AND J DAVIDSON
GRANDMA'S
NATURAL REMEDIES AND ANCIENT RECIPES
ALL 5 BOOKS IN 1
HEALTH LEARNING SERIES
DLJEEP J SINGH AND J DAVIDSON

Health Learning Series

- Amazing Health Benefits of Intermittent Fasting
- What Makes Me Fat? How to eliminate obesity naturally!
- Natural Cures of Anxiety
- Medical Conditions Requiring Paleo Diet
- How to Eliminate Heart Burn and Acid Reflux Naturally
- Eliminate Pain! How to get rid of arthritis and joint pain naturally!
- Ways to Improve Self-Esteem
- How to Avoid Brain Aging Dementia - Memory Loss Naturally
- Paleo Diet Side Effects
- Paleo Diet Good or Bad? An Analysis of Arguments and Counter-Arguments
- How to Get Rid of High Blood Pressure or Hypertension Naturally
- Health Benefits of Meditation
- Paleo Diet For Weight Loss
- Paleo Diet for Athletes
- How to Reduce the Chances of a Heart Attack
- How to Get Rid of Asthma Naturally

Amazing Animal Book Series

A Beginner's Guide to Rock Gardens — Page 42

Learn To Draw Series

How to Build and Plan Books

Entrepreneur Book Series

Our books are available at

1. Amazon.com
2. Barnes and Noble
3. Itunes
4. Kobo
5. Smashwords
6. Google Play Books

Publisher

JD-Biz Corp

P O Box 374

Mendon, Utah 84325

http://www.jd-biz.com/